Ellis Island Guide

with Lower Manhattan

by Oscar Israelowitz

TO BEV + SY

BEST WISHES

FROM

Oscar 11/4/90

Israelowitz Publishing

P.O.Box 228 Brooklyn, New York 11229 Tel. (718) 951-7072

Library of Congress Catalogue Card Number: 90-083282
International Standard Book Number: 1-878741-01-2

Printed in the United States.

Cover Photo
Italian immigrants arriving at Ellis Island.
Photo Credit: Lewis W. Hine
International Museum of Photography: George Eastman House

Contents

How to Get to Ellis Island

From Manhattan:

By car:

 From the west side of Manhattan, take West Street south to Battery Park. From the east side of Manhattan, take the FDR Drive to Battery Park exit (State Street). Don't go under the tunnel. Park the car and walk to Castle Clinton National Memorial (the old circular brownstone structure in the middle of the park). Purchase a ticket for the ferry to Ellis Island inside Castle Clinton. It is about a ten-minute ride out to Ellis Island.

There is free street parking on Saturdays and Sundays only. Other times, park your car in the public parking lots nearby. There is an inexpensive high-rise parking facilty (Battery Parking Garage) located on Greenwich Street (near Rector Street).

By subway:

Take the IRT Lexington Avenue Line (#4 or #5) to Bowling Green.

Take the IRT Seventh Avenue Line (#1/9) to South Ferry (and note the exquisite wall bas reliefs in the station).

Take the BMT N or R Line to Whitehall Street.

By bus:

M1 to South Ferry (weekdays only).

M6 to South Ferry.

M15 to South Ferry.

From New Jersey:

Take the New Jersey Turnpike to Exit 14B (Liberty State Park).
Follow the signs to the Statue of Liberty/Ellis Island (Circle Line)
Ferry Service Dock which is located near the historic landmark
Central Railroad of New Jersey (CRRNJ) Terminal. The ferry ride
from this point is about five minutes.

Ellis Island

Ellis Island is located in the Upper New York Bay approximately 1500 feet east of Jersey City, New Jersey. The original 3.3 acre island was called "Oyster Island" by the Dutch Burghers since it was there that they shucked and ate the oysters from the clear waters nearby. The British took possession of the region in 1664 and renamed it "Gull Island" and later called it "Gibbet Island." This was the site of executions of a number of pirates in the 18th century. The term "Gibbet" refers to the gallows tree.

In the late 18th century, the island was sold to a New York businessman, Samuel Ellis. In 1808, the island was sold to New York State and then sold to the Federal Government. It was during this period, before the War of 1812, that harbor defenses were built on Governors, Bedloes, and Ellis Island.

During the Civil War, the Navy Department used Ellis Island as a munitions arsenal. There were enough explosives on the island to destroy all of New York, Brooklyn, Staten Island and Jersey City.

Castle Clinton was built on landfill just south of Battery Park, Manhattan. It was designed as a fort which would protect New York harbor against the invading British forces. The structure was closed down as a fortress and converted into a concert hall which seated approximately 6,000. It was called Castle Garden. A Swedish opera star, Jenny Lind, was introduced by P.T. Barnum in this concert hall. She later became popular as the "Swedish Nightingale." From 1855 to 1890, Castle Garden served as the immigration processing center.

In 1891, Castle Garden was closed down as an immigration processing center. The number of immigrants coming in grew daily, causing a breakdown of the entire process of inspection and making it impossible for the authorities to keep white slavers and "con" men away from the incoming immigrants.

Congress selected Ellis Island to serve as the immigration depot. It removed the munitions dump, enlarged the island with landfill and constructed a large three-story reception center, a hospital, and generating plant. Most of these structures were constructed of resinous Georgia pine and spruce and sheathed with galvanized iron. The new Ellis Island Immigration Station was officially dedicated on New Year's Day, 1892. It was designed to permit the entry of up to 10,000 immigrants per day.

On the evening of June 14, 1897, a fire of undisclosed origin completely destroyed all of the wooden structures on Ellis Island. The immigrants who were on the island at the time were all safely evacuated to New York City. There were no injuries, however, all of the immigration records from 1855 to 1897 were completely destroyed.

From 1897 to 1900, the Barge Office in Battery Park was used to process all immigrants. During this period new fireproof red brick and ironwork buildings were constructed on Ellis Island. They were trimmed with Indiana limestone and Maine granite and were designed by the architectural firm of Boring & Tilton. The main building was designed in the French Renaissance style. The building measured 338 feet long, 168 feet wide, and 100 feet high with four turrets which housed stair-wells and elevators. During the recent restoration project, building inspectors discovered that the two original "bird-cage" elevators built by Otis Elevator Company were "under-designed." It seems, that during construction of the Main Arrivals Building, the original engineers were bribed and accepted these poorly designed elevators.

The first floor contained a baggage room for new arrivals,

The steerage crowds huddled between their boxes and bales.
(Photo Credit: National Parks Service)

administrative offices, a large railroad room, and a very wide stairway which lead to the central part of the Main Registry Hall on the second floor where the actual processing of immigrants occurred. The expanded facilities were designed to process 500,000 immigrants per year. The planners did not anticipate catastrophic events in Europe such as the pogroms in Russia and the subsequent arrival of over one million immigrants in 1907. The maximum number of immigrants processed on Ellis Island was on April 17, 1907. 11,747 immigrants were processed on that one day. Between 1892 and 1954, twelve million immigrants were processed. Another five million immigrants' paperwork was prossessed on Ellis Island. Ninety-eight per cent of immigrants were permitted entry via Ellis Island, only 2% were sent back to the "old country."

COMING TO AMERICA

The United States has been referred to as the "Golden Land," where the streets are paved with gold. This dream and hope brought millions of immigrants to the shores of America. Many were fleeing religious persecution, despotic regimes, or severe poverty. The poem written by Emma Lazarus, *The New Colossus*, has been the welcoming statement for these impoverished immigrants. It has been enshrined at the base of the Statue of Liberty:

"Give me your tired, your poor,
Your huddled masses yearning to breathe free,
The wretched refuse of your teeming shore,
Send these, the homeless, the tempest-tost to me,
I lift my lamp beside the golden door."

The majority of the immigrants who came to America between 1855 and 1921 could not afford cabin-class on the steamship lines. Instead, they would pay as much as $30 per person for the ocean voyage by steerage.

A steerage berth was an iron bunk with a mattress of straw and no pillow. The floors of the compartments were made of wood, which were swept every morning and sprinkled with sand. Two washrooms were provided for the steerage class, and both were used by both sexes at the same time. There was a small basin and a dishpan plus some other cans that were used as laundry tubs. Since most of the metal cans were used for washing, there was a shortage of receptacles to use in case of seasickness. Thus, as the voyage progressed, the conditions became more filthy and more unbearable.

During the twelve days across the ocean, only the salt breeze overcame the odors. And by the end of the journey, everything was dirty and disagreeable. On rough passages, the conditions were far worse, because the decks were filled with vomit and there was no provision for personal cleanliness. Before docking, immigrants were given presents by the steamship company; each woman was given a piece of candy and each man a pipe and tobacco.

The first glimpse of America was the Statue of Liberty in New York harbor. All of the immigrants changed into their "Sunday best" before they left the ship. Many donned their colorful folk costumes, they wanted to make a good impression during their inspections on Ellis Island.

As the ship passed through the Narrows into the New York harbor it was approached by a small cutter. A uniformed inspector would board the ship and look at the list of first-class passengers and visually "inspect" the second-class passengers. He would then ask the ship's doctor if there were any contagious diseases on board. If the answer was positive, the entire crew and passengers would be

Immigrants arriving on Ellis Island.   (Photo Credit: National Park Service)

isolated at the Quarantine Station at Staten Island or at Hoffman or Swinburne Islands (located just south of the Narrows).

If the ship was "cleared for entry" the passengers were separated. The first and second class passengers were permitted to enter directly at the piers where the ship docked. The steerage passengers, however, were transferred to a shuttle barge which took them to Ellis Island for processing.

PROCESSING OF IMMIGRANTS

Before leaving the ship, the immigrants in steerage class were given a tag which had their name, country of origin and a number. They stepped off the ferry onto the pier in front of the Main Arrivals Building. They walked under the canopy carrying luggage which contained their worldly possessions. They brought bags, boxes, trunks, wooden containers and wicker baskets. Their main concern was that these meager treasures might be lost or stolen. The first encounter in the Main Arrivals Building was the Baggage Room. Many immigrants refused to part with their luggage even when it was guarded by the baggage clerks. There was also a language problems since the majority of the immigrants spoke little or no English.

Ellis Island represented a traumatic event in the lives of most of the 17 million immigrants who were processed there. It represented a chaotic nightmare. Family members could be separated with some accepted and others rejected. The painful decision of whether to stay or return with a loved one had to be made on the spot. It is estimated that there were three thousand suicides on Ellis Island. However, of the 17 million immigrants who were processed on Ellis Island, 98% were admitted.

From the Baggage Room below, the immigrants were led upstairs

Ferries arriving at Ellis Island in 1905.   (Photo Credit: National Park Service)

The dreaded eye examination on Ellis Island.
(Photo Credit: Library of Congress)

into the large arena of the Registry Hall. They were examined in groups of thirty. As the immigrants reached the top of the stairs the physical examination started. This exam might take an hour or several days, depending on whether or not the individual was confined to the station's hospital.

As the immigrants passed by, the doctors would look for signs of illness, such as lumps, fatigue, short wind. The doctors would write on the immigrant's lapel or shoulder or on a tag various letters of the alphabet: "L" meaning lung problem, "H" heart disease, and "X" indicating a possible lunatic or one with a mental problem. If the immigrants were deported, it would be at the expense of the steamship lines, since it was their obligation to check each passenger at the home port. At this point the eyes were checked, particularly for a contagious disease - trachoma.

If the immigrants survived the physical examination, they were taken to the Registry section to be interviewed. In all, there were as many as 29 questions. Your name? How did you pay for your passage? Do you have promise of a job? Are you an anarchist? Are you going to join a relative or friend? What is your address? Occupation? Where were you born? Have you ever been in a prison or in the poorhouse? Not all inspectors asked all 29 questions, and some inspectors by failing to ask all the questions missed certain cases of irregularities that were picked up later on in the process line.

The first question, "Your name?" was often a great problem for the immigrants. The inspectors sometimes could not understand what the immigrants were saying. It was at this point where the immigrants experienced a "name change." A German Jew became flustered at the questions of the inspector, and when he was asked his name, he answered, "Ich vergessen" (I forget). The inspector, who happened to be Irish misinterpreted these words and wrote the immigrant's name as Sean Ferguson. On other occasions, inspectors would tell the immigrants that their names were too long and that they would have to shorten them in order to "make it in America." An Italian told the inspector questioning him that his name was Mastroianni. His name was changed to Mister Yanni. He had to add a first name later for the official records.

Once the immigrants were given a "clean bill of health," the next step was downstairs to the money exchange office where marks, drachmas, lira, zloty, and kroner were traded for U.S. dollars. The entire processing of an immigrant took an average of six hours. During that period no meals or snacks were served by the immigration inspectors. Many of the immigrants brought food along from the ocean liner. Jewish immigrants who only ate kosher food would often bring their food supplies from the "Old Country." The only way an immigrant could get a free meal was if he was detained for an irregularity in his documents or for health problems by the immigration inspectors.

The railroad agent was the last stop before the immigrants headed for all parts of the country. One third of all immigrants took the ferry across the river to Manhattan's Lower East Side. Others were told in the "Old Country" to purchase a railroad ticket to "Springfield, America!" They didn't realize that there are no less than fourteen "Springfields" scattered throughout the United States. This is how immigrants ended up in Springfield, Illinois, New Jersey, Massachusetts, and North Carolina. One poor immigrant wanted to get to Houston Street, on the Lower East Side of Manhattan. The ticket clerk sold him a ticket to Houston, Texas! Some ticket agents on Ellis Island took advantage of the immigrants. They charged two or three times the legal price of railroad tickets. Others told the immigrants who purchased tickets to Chicago that they had to change in San Francisco, California to catch the train to Chicago!

Following World War I, many Americans were eager to see

The Registry Room circa 1921.   (Photo Credit: National Park Service)

immigration restriction. The war had rekindled a fear of foreigners. The Immigration Acts of 1917, 1921, 1924, and 1929 virtually ended the vast flows of immigrants into this country. Ellis Island was then used as a Coast Guard station and later as a detention center for enemy aliens. In November, 1954, Ellis Island was declared surplus property by the General Services Administration and was officially closed. In 1965, Ellis Island was designated as a part of the Statue of Liberty National Monument. It is presently under the auspices of the National Park Service.

Ellis Island originally measured 3.3 acres but was enlarged by landfill. Island number two was added to the southwest of the original island in 1902. It was separated from island one by a ferry slip and contained the hospital buildings. Island number three was added in 1909 and contained the contagious disease hospital. Ellis Island was enlarged to 27.5 acres. The new ferry building was built as a WPA project in the 1930s. It was designed in the Art Deco style.

After 1924, with the legislation of stringent immigration policies, Ellis Island became primarily a center for the detention and deportation of aliens who had entered the country illegally or had violated the terms of their admission. During World War II, Ellis Island was used as a Coast Guard station and was a detention center for suspected Nazi spies. The island was officially closed on November 29, 1954.

Aerial view of Ellis Island. (Photo credit: National Park Service)

Hungarian family arriving at Ellis Island ca. 1910.   (Photo Credit: National Park Service)

Ellis Island - Historic Dates

1630. The Colonial governors of Nieuw Amsterdam purchase a small, 3.5-acre mudbank in Upper New York Bay, near the New Jersey shore. The Indians called it Kioshk, or Gull Island, after the birds that were its only inhabitants. The Dutch settlers called it "Oyster Island," after the many surrounding oyster beds. The island barely rose above the surface at high tide.

1700s. During Colonial period, the Island was known as Dyre's, then Bucking.

1776. By the time of the American Revolution, the Island was owned by Samuel Ellis, a New York merchant and owner of a small tavern on the Island catering to fisherman.

1808. Samuel Ellis' heirs sold the Island to New York State. The name Ellis Island stuck. Later in the year, the Federal Government bought Ellis Island for $10,000.

1812. Ellis Island served as an arsenal during the War of 1812.

1834. By the terms of an interstate agreement, Ellis Island and neighboring Bedloe's Island (renamed Liberty Island in 1956, site of the Statue of Liberty) were declared part of New York State, even though both islands are on the New Jersey side of the main ship channel.

1890. The States turned over control of immigration to the Federal Government. The U.S. Congress appropriated $75,000 to build the first Federal Immigration Station on Ellis Island. Artesian wells were dug, and landfill (from incoming ships' ballast and New York City subway tunnels) doubled the size of Ellis Island to over six acres. While the new immigration station was under construction, the Barge Office at the Battery on the tip of Manhattan, was used for immigrant reception.

1892. The first Ellis Island Immigration Station was officially opened on January 1, 1892. On the first day, three large ships were waiting to land, and 700 immigrants passed through Ellis Island. In the first year, nearly 450,000 immigrants passed through the Island.

On January 1, Annie Moore, a 15 year old girl from County Cork, Ireland, is the first person admitted to the new immigration station. She is greeted by officials and given a $10.00 gold piece.

1897. On June 15, fire breaks out in one of the towers of the main building. The roof collapses. There are 200 immigrants on the island but miraculously no lives are lost. Regrettably, all immigration records are destroyed, some of which date to 1840 and the Castle Garden era. The Immigration Station is moved back to the Barge Office in Battery Park.

1900. The December 17 issue of *The New York Tribune* describes the Battery facility as "grimy, gloomy...more suggestive of an enclosure for animals than a receiving station for prospective citizens of the United States." The rebuilt receiving station on Ellis Island, designed by Boring & Tilton (a New York architectural firm) is officially opened in December. It is constructed of red brick with limestone trim and completely fireproof. 2,251 people pass through on opening day.

1901. Teddy Roosevelt becomes President and begins work on cleaning up Ellis Island operation.

1902. William Williams is appointed Commissioner of Immigration. He institutes a clean sweep and awards contracts on the basis of merit announcing contracts would be revoked the moment any dishonesty was suspected. He posts "Kindness and Consideration" signs and imposes penalties for any violation of this rule. The father of Lee Iacocca is processed through Ellis Island this year.

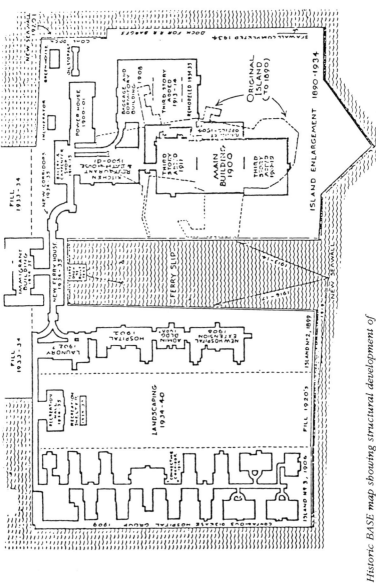

Historic BASE map showing structural development of

Ellis Island from 1890-1935.

The Immigrant Dining Room could accommodate 1200 people.   (Photo Credit: National Park Service)

1907. This was the peak year at Ellis Island with 1,004,756 immigrants received. The all-time daily high was 11,747 on April 17, 1907.

1908. The Baggage and Dormitory Building was completed and capacity of the hospital was doubled. A dining room for 1,000 at a sitting was built on the top floor of the Kitchen and Laundry Building.

1916. On July 30, New Jersey's Black Tom Wharves, just west of Liberty Island, are blown up by German saboteurs. Crates of ammunitions and 18 barges destined for Russia (then at war with Germany) are set ablaze. The explosions last for hours and plate glass windows, as far uptown as Times Square, are shattered. Burning debris showers Ellis Island. Over 600 people are on hand and miraculously, none are harmed. Damage is estimated at $400,000.00.

The most notable addition in the repairs was the new ceiling over the Great Hall, a barrel vault constructed by the Guastavino Brothers.

1917. Ellis Island becomes a detention center for enemy aliens; a way station for Navy personnel; and a hospital for the Army. The literacy test is introduced, meaning anyone over the age of 16 who could not read 30 to 40 test words in their own language or dialect was excluded. This stipulation would stay on the books until 1952.

1918. The U.S. Army took over most of Ellis Island for use as a way station and treatment of returning sick and wounded American servicemen. During the war, there was a sharp decline in immigration as the numbers of newcomers passing through Ellis Island decreased from 178,416 in 1915, to 28,867 in 1918.

1921. Post-war immigration quickly revived and 560,971 immigrants passed through Ellis Island in 1921. The first Immigration Quota Law passed the U.S. Congress.

1924. The Immigration Act of 1924 further restricted immigration, reducing the annual quota to some 164,000. This marked the end of mass immigration to America. The buildings at Ellis Island began to fall into disuse and disrepair.

1930s. Funds from the Public Works Administration permitted the landfill addition of recreation grounds on the Manhattan side of the Main Building. Works Progress Administration (WPA) labor added landscaping, new playgrounds and gardens on the new landfill. Ellis Island reached its present 27.5 acres.

1939-1945. During World War II, Ellis Island facilities were used by the Coast Guard to house and train recruits. After the U.S. entered the war in December, 1941, Ellis Island was used as a detention center for suspected enemy aliens and as a hospital for returning wounded servicemen.

1950. A brief flurry of activity occurred on Ellis Island after the passage of the Internal Security Act of 1950, which excluded arriving aliens who had been members of Communist and Fascist organizations. Remodeling and repairs were performed on the buildings to accommodate detainees who numbered as many as 1,500 at one time.

1952. As a result of the Immigration and Naturalization Act of 1952 and a liberalized detention policy, the number of detainees on Ellis Island dropped to less than 30.

1954. All thirty-three structures on Ellis Island were officially closed in November, 1954. Ellis Island was placed under the jurisdiction of the General Services Administration from 1954 to 1965.

1965. President Lyndon B. Johnson issued Proclamation 3656 adding Ellis Island to the Statue of Liberty National Monument, thus placing Ellis Island under the jurisdiction of the National Park Service.

1976. Ellis Island was opened to the public for visits. Over 50,000 people visited the Island that year.

1984. Restoration of Ellis Island started.

1990. Restoration of Main Arrivals Building completed.

Number of Immigrants Arriving in United States by Nationality

1850 - 1948

Czech 1,000,000

Danish 338,085

Dutch 372,384

Finnish 284,240

French 624,561

German 6,064,653

Greek 434,418

Hungarian 662,068

Irish 4,597,429

Italian 4,752,735

Jewish 5,000,000

Norwegian 800,000

Polish 2,905,859

Romanian 158,208

Swedish 1,200,000

Russian 3,300,000

Yugoslavian 383,393

Total: 32,888,033

Source:"Immigration & Naturalization Systems of the United States 81st Congressional Senate Report 1515" April 20, 1950.

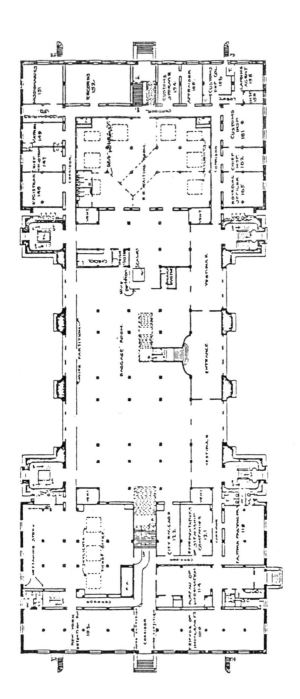

Original first floor plan of Main Arrivals Building.

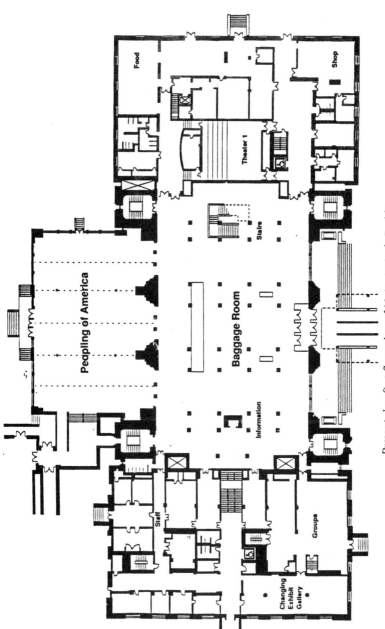

Present-day first floor plan of Main Arrivals Building.

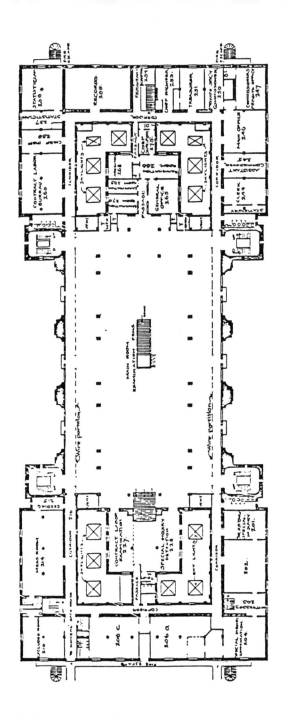

Original second floor plan of Main Arrivals Building.

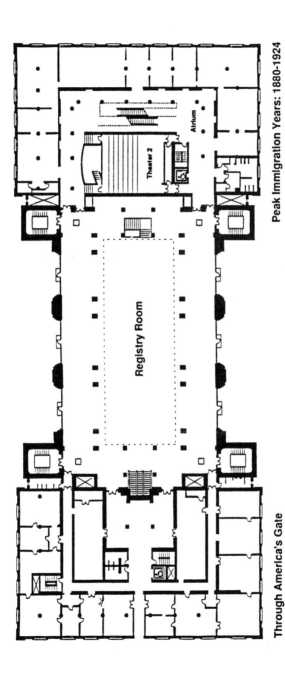

Registry Room

Theater 2

Atrium

Present-day second floor plan of Main Arrivals Building.

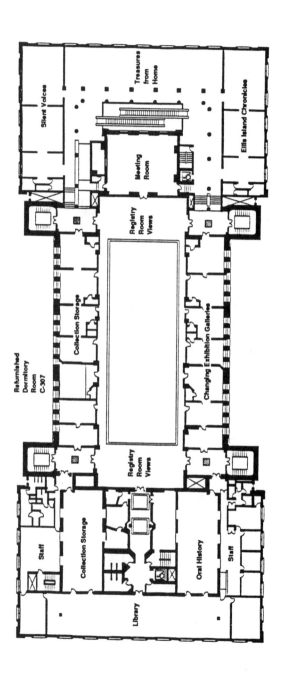

Present-day third floor plan of Main Arrivals Building.

Main Arrivals Building before restoration.

Main Arrivals Building before restoration.

Immigrants arriving on Ellis Island. (Photo Credit: Museum of the City of New York)

Newly-restored Registry Room.

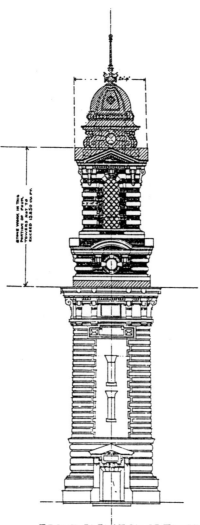

FRONT ELEVATION OF TOWERS.
SCALE ⅛"—1'.

Architectural detail on front façade of Main Arrivals Building.

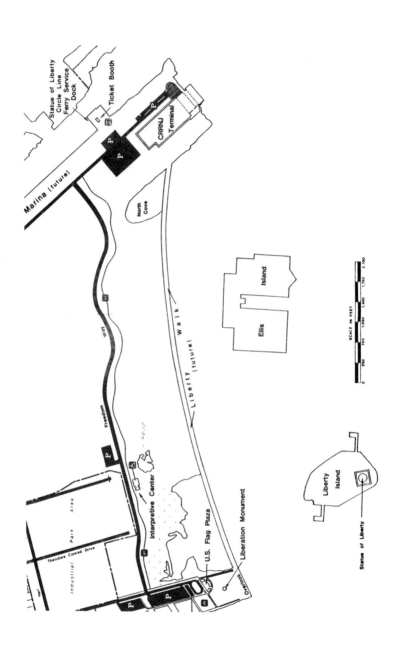

Statue of Liberty
Circle Line
Ferry Service
Dock

Ticket Booth

Marina (future)

CRRNJ Terminal

North Cove

Freedom Way

Liberty Walk (future)

Theodore Conrad Drive

Industrial Park Area

Interpretive Center

U.S. Flag Plaza

Liberation Monument

Overlook

Ellis Island

SCALE IN FEET

0   350   700   1,050   1,400   1,750   2,100

Liberty Island

Statue of Liberty

Liberty State Park

Jersey City, New Jersey

CENTRAL RAILROAD OF NEW JERSEY TERMINAL

On the New York Harbor, less than 2,000 feet from the Statue of Liberty, Liberty State Park has served a vital role in the development of New Jersey's metropolitan region and the history of the nation.

During the 19th and early 20th centuries the area that is now Liberty State Park was a major waterfront industrial area with an extensive freight and passenger transportation network. This network became the lifeline of New York City and the harbor area. The heart of this transportation network was the Central Railroad of New Jersey (CRRNJ) Terminal, which is now located in the northern portion of the park.

From 1892 through 1954, the CRRNJ Terminal stood with the Statue of Liberty and Ellis Island to unfold one of this nation's most dramatic stories: the immigration of Northern, Southern and Eastern Europeans into the United States. After being greeted by the Statue of Liberty and processed at Ellis Island, these immigrants purchased tickets at the Terminal and boarded trains that took them to their new homes throughout the United States.

The CRRNJ Terminal was constructed in 1889. In 1914, as many as 28,000 people passed through the terminal daily. Over 10 million immigrants set foot on mainland U.S. soil for the first time at the CRRNJ Terminal.

During World War I, the southern area of today's Liberty State Park served as a munitions depot for our armed forces. This was the site of the famous Black Tom explosion in 1916. The explosion, which is believed to have been an act of sabotage, involved freight cars of munitions bound for Europe and the Allied Forces.

The 1950s and '60s brought an end to the railroad activities in this area. As a result, the railroad facilities and land were abandoned. Liberty State Park was formally opened on Flag Day, June 14, 1976, as New Jersey's bicentennial gift to the nation.

Ferries to the Statue of Liberty and Ellis Island are located near the old Central Railroad of New Jersey Terminal. For ferry information call (212) 269-5755 or (201) 435-9499.

LIBERATION MONUMENT

The Liberation Monument was designed by the noted sculptor, Nathan Rapaport. The 30-foot-high bronze monument portrays an American soldier carrying a concentration camp victim. The victim's are is tattooed with the concentration camp number. The monument's location, just behind the Statue of Liberty and in view of Manhattan's skyline, makes this one of the most moving Holocaust memorials in the world!

How to get there:

By car...Take the New Jersey Turnpike to Exit 14B. After the exit, just follow the signs which are located about 100 feet from the toll booths.

By train...Take the PATH train (at the World Trade Center, in Manhattan) to Exchange Place, then take the local bus or a taxi.

Holocaust Memorial in Liberty State Park.

Lower Manhattan

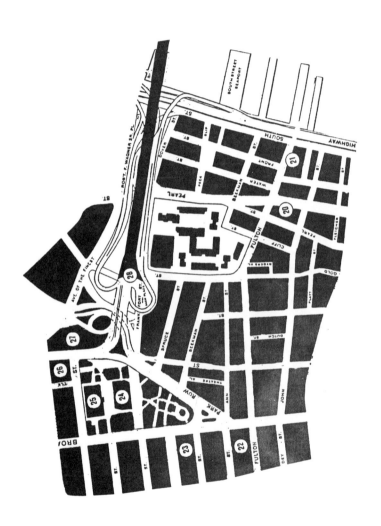

CASTLE CLINTON NATIONAL MONUMENT   *Stop 1.*

Battery Park
Subway: IRT #1/9 to South Ferry

Castle Clinton is a product of the Napoleonic era. The conflict between France and Great Britain plus the English policy of seizing American ships and impressing American seamen into the British Navy produced months of tension. The climax came on June 22, 1807, with the British attack upon the American frigate *Chesapeake.* In New York, mass meetings denounced the attack. At the same time, a great "fortification fever" swept the city, for New York, except for Fort Columbus on Governors Island, was virtually defenseless.

In short order five new forts were built: Fort Wood on Bedloes Island, Fort Gibson on Ellis Island, three-tiered Castle Williams on Governors Island, the South-west Battery at the tip of Manhattan Island, and the North Battery at the foot of Hubert Street.

Circular in shape, the South-west Battery stood in about 35 feet of water, 200 feet from shore. A timber causeway with drawbridge connected the new fort to Manhattan. The South-west Battery had 28 guns on one tier. Inside the rounded ends of the rear wall, on the land side, were the magazines. Quarters for the officers were at each side of the passageway to the causeway. No barracks for the enlisted men existed.

The South-west Battery was completed in 1811. Throughout the War of 1812 the fort stood ready, but its guns fired at nothing more dangerous than a harmless hulk moored in the river for target practice. At the end of the war, the fort was named Castle Clinton in honor of DeWitt Clinton, a former mayor of New York City and later governor of New York State. In 1823, Castle Clinton was ceded to New York City. The following year it was leased by the city as a place of public entertainment.

Castle Clinton Immigration Depot.

Opened as Castle Garden on July 3, 1824, it soon became one of the favored "places of resort" in New York. The interior was described as a "fanciful garden, tastefully ornamented with shrubs and flowers." In time, a great fountain was installed. The Garden was the setting for band concerts, fireworks, an occasional balloon ascension, and demonstrations of the latest scientific achievements. The gun rooms, decorated with marble busts and painted panoramas, became a promenade. The officers' quarters became a bar selling choice liquors, confections, and ice.

In the 1840s, Castle Garden was roofed over and more serious entertainment was added to the fare. The Garden then presented operas, in concert form. On September 11, 1850, P.T. Barnum presented the "Swedish Nightingale," Jenny Lind, in her American debut. More than 6,000 people filled Castle Garden for that concert.

On August 3, 1855, Castle Garden, under lease to the State of New York, was opened as an immigrant landing depot. Between 1855 and 1889, more than eight million immigrants - two out of every three persons immigrating to the United States in this period - passed through the Garden. Castle Garden was closed as an immigration depot on April 18, 1890.

In 1896, Castle Clinton was once again altered, this time to become the New York City Aquarium. The Aquarium was moved to Coney Island in 1941.

Today, Castle Clinton has been restored to its 1811 fort design. It is a national historic monument and is administered by the National Park Service. There is a small museum with 3-D scale models of the transformations of Castle Clinton from 1811 to the twentieth century.

The kiosk on the old parade grounds of the fort sells tickets for the ferries to the Statue of Liberty and Ellis Island. For ticket information call (212) 269-5755.

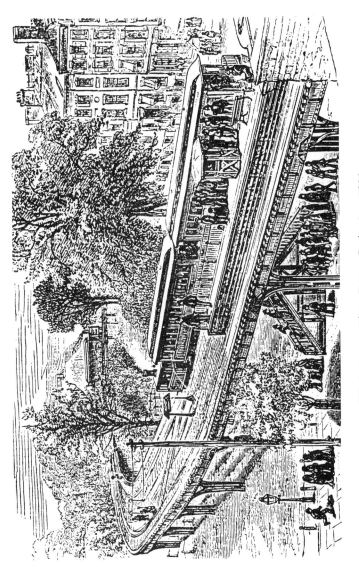

Ninib Avenue "El" in Battery Park, circa 1890.

EMMA LAZARUS WALK   *Stop 2.*

Battery Park
Subway: IRT #4, 5 to Bowling Green

The walkway from Bowling Green to Castle Clinton was once a plank bridge in the water connecting Manhattan to the fortress island. Battery Park was created with landfill. The walkway was named after the Emma Lazarus, a Jewish poetess and descendant of the Reverend Gershom Mendes Seixas, minister of the Spanish and Portuguese Synagogue and Revolutionary War patriot. She wrote her sonnet, *The New Colossus*, which is affixed to the base of the Statue of Liberty. There is a replica of that sonnet near the Fireboat Station in Battery Park.

BOWLING GREEN   *Stop 3.*

Subway: IRT #4, 5 to Bowling Green

Erected by the Common Council in 1771. A fence surrounds New York's earliest park. The park was leased in 1783 for use as a Bowling Green at a rental of one peppercorn a year. Patriots, who in 1776 destroyed an equestrian statue of George III which stood here, are said to have removed the crowns which capped the fence posts but the fence itself remains.

NO. ONE BROADWAY   *Stop 4.*

Subway: IRT #4, 5 to Bowling Green

Adjoining this site was the first Dutch fort on Manhattan Island known as Fort New Amsterdam. The first house was erected here before 1664. In 1771 Captain Archibald Kennedy built here his residence which was used in 1776 by General Washington as his headquarters and later by General Howe during the British

A stock broker "stranded" on the frozen East River following the Great Blizzard of 1888.

New York's first subway station lies under City Hall.

occupation. It was later used as a hotel but was torn down. In 1882 it was replaced by the Washington Building which was transformed in 1920-21 into the International Mercantile Marine Company and known as No. One Broadway.

SUBWAY KIOSK *Stop 5.*

Subway: IRT #4, 5 to Bowling Green - south end

The Interborough Rapid Transit (IRT) was financed by the banker August Belmont ("Belmont" is the French translation of the German name, "Schonberg"- beautiful mountain). Belmont specified that the new subway should be decorated with ornate mosaic tiles, ceramic works of art, and beautiful name entablatures. Each station was to be designed in a unique motif. This aided many hundreds of thousands of newly-arrived immigrants who could not read. So when they arrived at the South Ferry station for example, they saw the terra-cotta bas relief of a sloop. They then knew that they had to get off the train at that picture.

The masonry kiosk was designed in 1905 by Heins & La Farge in the Beaux Arts style. It has recently been restored.There are two additional subway kiosks in the city. One is located at Broadway and 72nd Street. The other is located in Brooklyn, at the Atlantic Avenue (and Flatbush junction) station.

U.S. CUSTOM HOUSE *Stop 6.*

Bowling Green at State, Whitehall & Bridge Streets
Subway: IRT #4, 5 to Bowling Green

The U.S. Custom House was designed in 1907 by Cass Gilbert in the Beaux-Arts style. The four heroic sculptures were created by Daniel Chester French. The splendid oval rotunda contains murals by Reginald Marsh, commissioned as a WPA project in the 1930s.

There were plans of using this building as the New Holocaust Memorial. It seemed that the building was too "ornate" for such a use. At this point, the U.S. Customs House is not open to the public. The lower floors are used as a Bankruptcy Court.

JERUSALEM GROVE   *Stop 7.*

Battery Park
Subway: IRT #4, 5 to Bowling Green

In honor of the United States' Bicentennial in 1976, the mayor of Jerusalem, Teddy Kolleck, presented the City of New York and then Mayor Abraham Beame, with fifteen Atlas cedars. The stone bearing this historical presentation lies in the grass near the Fireboat Station. The memorial is inscribed on Jerusalem limestone (Dolomite). The city ordinance in Jerusalem requires all structures in that city to be constructed with Jerusalem limestone.

WORLD FINANCIAL CENTER   *Stop 8.*

Battery Park City
Subway: IRT # 1/9 to Rector Street

Battery Park City consists of 92 acres of landfill. Much of this landfill comes from the excavations for the World Trade Center. The 14-acre World Financial Center was built by the Toronto-based Olympia & York Company.

The World Financial Center was designed by architect Cesar Pelli. The glazed Wintergarden is a grand public space comparable in size to Grand Central Station in New York. It has restaurants at its sides, and a grand staircase at its east forming a natural amphitheater for watching not only performances but the Hudson River as well.

The steel structure recalls industrialized structures of the 19th century. Sixteen palm trees. Sixteen palm trees, selected for having

U.S. Custom House was designed in 1907 by Cass Gilbert.

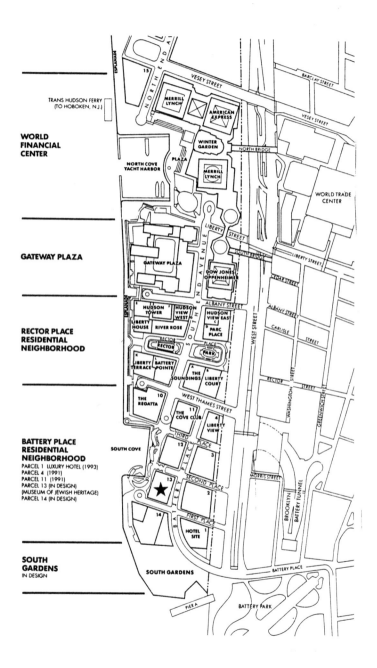

WORLD FINANCIAL CENTER

GATEWAY PLAZA

RECTOR PLACE RESIDENTIAL NEIGHBORHOOD

BATTERY PLACE RESIDENTIAL NEIGHBORHOOD
PARCEL 1 LUXURY HOTEL (1993)
PARCEL 4 (1991)
PARCEL 11 (1991)
PARCEL 13 (IN DESIGN)
(MUSEUM OF JEWISH HERITAGE)
PARCEL 14 (IN DESIGN)

SOUTH GARDENS
IN DESIGN

Within map:

ESPLANADE
TRANS HUDSON FERRY (TO HOBOKEN, N.J.)
NORTH END AVENUE
15
VESEY STREET
BARCLAY STREET
MERRILL LYNCH
AMERICAN EXPRESS
VESEY STREET
WINTER GARDEN
NORTH BRIDGE
PLAZA
NORTH COVE YACHT HARBOR
MERRILL LYNCH
WORLD TRADE CENTER
LIBERTY STREET
SOUTH END AVENUE
GATEWAY PLAZA
DOW JONES OPPENHEIMER
LIBERTY STREET
CEDAR STREET
ALBANY STREET
ALBANY STREET
HUDSON TOWER
HUDSON VIEW WEST
HUDSON VIEW EAST
WEST STREET
CARLISLE STREET
LIBERTY HOUSE
RIVER ROSE
PARC PLACE
RECTOR PLACE
RECTOR
PARK
RECTOR STREET
LIBERTY TERRACE
BATTERY POINTE
THE SOUNDINGS
LIBERTY COURT
WASHINGTON STREET
GREENWICH STREET
WEST THAMES STREET
10 THE REGATTA
11 THE COVE CLUB
4 LIBERTY VIEW
THIRD PLACE
SOUTH COVE
12
3
SECOND PLACE
MORRIS STREET
13
2
BROOKLYN BATTERY TUNNEL
BATTERY PLACE
14
FIRST PLACE
HOTEL SITE 1
SOUTH GARDENS
BATTERY PLACE
PIER A
BATTERY PARK

foliage only above eye level at the Wintergarden's second story, will grow in aerated soil and with the help of grow lamps. The 45-foot-high palm trees were brought from the Mohave Desert in California and can resist the low winter humidity, unlike tropical palms.

To accommodate the planters, the area beneath the Wintergarden, which includes New Jersey PATH trains and, in fact, water from the Hudson River, had to be elaborately restructured. A "table" was built over the PATH trains. The Wintergarden "sits" on this concrete table.

There are more than 6 acres of marble in 27 different varieties in the lobby floors and some wall area, all of it hand-set by 50 stone cutters. An Italian quarry was even reopened to furnish one of the marbles. Both the gilt stenciled ceilings of the gatehouse building and the Scalamandre jacquard fabric on elevator core walls are examples of luxuries deemed worthwhile by Olympia & York's quality engineers.

Other major projects developed by Olympia & York include Toronto's Harbourfront and the Canary Wharf in London's East End.

MUSEUM OF JEWISH HERITAGE   *Stop 9.*
A LIVING MEMORIAL TO THE HOLOCAUST

Battery Park City (southern tip)
Subway: IRT #4, 5 to Bowling Green

New York honors the memory of the six million Jews who perished during the Holocaust. The Museum will be located along the water's edge at the southern end of Battery Park City, in view of the Statue of Liberty and Ellis Island. The Museum will contain permanent exhibitions on four main themes: The World Before, The Holocaust, The Aftermath, and Renewal in America. The path through the first three of these themes will be a journey - a rite of passage - from the warmth of European Jewish life in the early 20th century, through the pain and darkness of the Holocaust, into the light of liberation and the rebirth achieved in the Aftermath.

Museum-goers also will have an opportunity to explore the Museum's fourth theme, Renewal in America, which tells the saga of Jewish immigration to the United States from 1654 until today.

There will be a state-of-the-art Learning Center and a highly varied program of changing exhibitions.

Visitors enter the Museum through a 60-foot-high atrium. The permanent exhibitions begin with a sweeping treatment of Jewish dispersion in Europe over two millennia. This space also provides entry to a theater, where visitors will view a unique introductory film, an intrinsic part of the exhibition that can be seen only at the Museum. At its conclusion the screen walls open, creating a portal into the Museum's lower level and the journey through the World Before, the Holocaust, and the Aftermath.

The Museum complex is designed by the architectural firm of James Stewart Polshek and Partners. The permanent exhibitions and museum spaces are conceived and designed by Chermayeff & Geismar Associates, whose distinguished projects include the John F. Kennedy Library Museum and the exhibitions at Ellis Island and the Statue of Liberty.

The Living Memorial to the Holocaust will consist of a 60-foot high cube built of stone and translucent glass. Reflected in the waters of the harbor, this structure will glow throughout the night like an eternal flame.

The Museum of Jewish Heritage and A Living Memorial to the Holocaust are scheduled to be completed in 1992.

The Museum of Jewish Heritage in Battery Park City.

TRINITY CHURCH   *Stop 10.*

Broadway & Wall Street   Tel. (212) 602-0848
Subway: IRT #4, 5 to Wall Street

Trinity Church, one of the most historic buildings in the city, was established in 1697 by Royal Charter of King William III of England. Three churches have occupied the site on Broadway at the head of Wall Street. The first was opened in 1698, having been paid for by personal subscriptions and taxation of citizens regardless of creed (the Church of England was the colony's established religion). The original church, a modest structure with a small entrance porch, faced the Hudson River.

For seventy years Trinity Parish was the only Church of England Parish in Manhattan. The growing population was accommodated by the erection of St. George's Chapel in 1752 and St. Paul's Chapel in 1766.

Early in the Revolutionary War, the rector and the vestrymen, many of whom were Tories, closed Trinity Church to Washington's army chaplains. It was reopened briefly when the British occupied New York but was destroyed in the Great Fire of 1776. Its ruins became known as "Burnt Church."

After the War of Independence Trinity became part of the newly organized Protestant Episcopal Church in the U.S. In 1788 the second church was begun on the site, and two years later it was consecrated in the presence of President Washington. It stood until 1839, when heavy snows damaged the roof and the building was found to be structurally unsound.

The present Trinity Church was completed in 1846 from a design by architect Richard Upjohn. Its details are based on English Perpendicular Gothic prototypes. The spire was once the highest structure on the New York skyline. The tower contains ten bells; three

New York Stock Exchange with Trinity Church on right.

Federal Hall National Memorial

of the eight original bells (a gift from London in 1797) are still in use. The bronze doors were designed by architect Richard Morris Hunt.

The two-and-one-half acre churchyard was a burial ground even during the Dutch period. Buried here are Alexander Hamilton (first Secretary of the Treasury), Albert Gallatin (member of Congress and Secretary of the Treasury for Jefferson), Francis Lewis (the only signer of the Declaration of Independence buried in Manhattan), Captain James ("Don't give up the ship!") Lawrence, and Robert Fulton (a successful portrait painter as well as an inventor).

The Martyrs' Monument, a notable architectural feature of the churchyard, was erected in memory of the men who sacrificed their lives in the War of Independence.

FEDERAL HALL NATIONAL MEMORIAL   *Stop 11.*
26 Wall Street   Tel. (212) 264-8711
Subway: IRT # 2, 3, 4, 5 to Wall Street

Throughout the 18th century, this was the vital center of New York's greatest events. At this place, the government of the United States of America began to function on Wednesday, March 4, 1789. New York City was the first capital of the United States, and New York's City Hall - remodeled, enlarged, and renamed Federal Hall in honor of its new, national importance - was the first Capitol, the building in which Congress met for its first session, with the first Senate in one wing and the first House of Representatives in the other.

On April 30, 1789 George Washington took the oath of office on the balcony of Federal Hall and became the first President of the United States.

The original City Hall was built in 1703 at the north end of Broad Street. The city's population was less than 5,000, including 1,000 Indians and slaves. Wall Street, which ran from river to river, was the northern boundary of the thickly built up area. Except for City Hall, Trinity Church, and a handful of houses, everything had been built south of a protective wooden wall which was built by the Dutch in 1653. The British took down the wall, but the name, Wall Street, remains.

The old Federal Hall was in a state of ruins after 1812. In 1842, the U.S. Customs House was built on this site in Greek Revival style by Town & Davis, with John Frazee and Samuel Thompson. In 1862, it became the Subtreasury Building. In 1955, Federal Hall was established as a national memorial. It is administered by the National Park Service.

NEW YORK STOCK EXCHANGE *Stop 12.*
8 Broad Street Tel. (212) 656-5167
Subway: IRT #2, 3, 4, 5 to Wall Street

This central market place for the purchase and sale of securities was founded in 1792 by merchants who met daily beneath a buttonwood tree that grew nearby. Completed in 1903 from designs by George B. Post. Sculptors of pediment group were J.A.Q. Ward and Paul W. Bartlett.

There are free tours of the galleries.

BROAD STREET *Stop 13.*
Subway: IRT # 2, 3, 4, 5 to Wall Street

The Dutch settlers of New Amsterdam named this drainage and

shipping canal after its prototype in Amsterdam, the Heren Gracht. The historic plaque on the floor in front of the main entrance to 85 Broad Street depicts a map of the area as it appeared in 1660. The Heren Gracht went as far as today's Exchange Place. Today's Bridge Street is where an ancient bridge crossed over the canal. Stone Street was the first to be cobbled. Pearl Street was the shoreline filled with shells (Mother-of-Pearl). The original canal was filled 100 years before the American Revolution. Broad Street was so named because it was the "widest" street in the area.

FLAGPOLE - HISTORIC MARKER   *Stop 14.*

State Street & Peter Minuit Plaza
Subway: N, R to Whitehall Street

In commemoration of the first Jewish settlement in New York City, the copper marker states, "Erected by the State of New York to honor the memory of the twenty-three men, women and children who landed in September, 1654, and founded the first Jewish community in North America."

SUPREME COURT OF THE UNITED STATES   *Stop 15.*

Water & Broad Streets (southeast corner)
Subway: N, R to Whitehall Street

The Supreme Court of the United States was first convened at this site on February 2, 1740 in the Merchant's Exchange Building which formerly stood in the center of Broad Street. Chief Justice John Jay attended in black and scarlet robes, presided.

On November 3, 1789, the United States District Court also was convened here, following its establishment under the Judiciary Act of 1789, thus becoming the first court organized under sovereignty of the newly-formed national government. James Duane who served as mayor of New York following the British evacuation, was appointed by General Washington to sit as the First District U.S. Judge.

The Exchange Building, erected in 1795, was torn down in 1799.

FRAUNCES TAVERN   *Stop 16.*

54 Pearl Street   Tel. (212) 425-1776
Subway: IRT #4, 5 to Bowling Green

Fraunces Tavern was originally built as a residence by Stephan de Lancey in 1719. The mansion was converted into an inn which was later purchased by Samuel Fraunces, a West Indian innkeeper. In 1762 he opened the Queen's Head Tavern, which quickly became a gathering place for the Sons of Liberty and other patriots. A group of merchants met here in 1768 to establish the Chamber of Commerce.

During the Revolution, Samuel Fraunces was taken prisoner by the British. He spent the remainder of the war as a cook in the house of General James Robertson.

When the British evacuated the city on November 25, 1783 Governor Clinton hosted a celebration banquet at the tavern for George Washington and Chevalier de la Luzerne, France's Ambassador to the fledgling nation.

The tavern was also the scene of a more poignant gathering on December 1, 1783, when Washington met his officers here to bid them farewell. He then departed for Annapolis to resign his commission and return to his Mount Vernon home. In 1785, Samuel Fraunces sold the tavern. He was asked to join Washington's staff after Washington became President. The tavern was later used by the new nation's Department of Foreign Affairs and War Department.

In the end of the nineteenth century, the building was used as a meeting place for social, civil, and service organizations. It was damaged by fire three times. A flat roof was added in 1832 and two additional stories were added in 1852. In 1904 it was acquired by the

Sons of the Revolution and in 1907 it was reconstructed by architect William H. Mersereau.

Fraunces Tavern is today one of the city's most elegant restaurants. There is also a small museum on the second level.

FRAUNCES TAVERN BLOCK

The Fraunces Tavern block is a rare example of a complete block of 18th and 19th century buildings that has survived Lower Manhattan's successive waves of construction.

The block was under water when The Strand, or Pearl Street, was the original shorefront. The small stream that flowed down what is presently Broad Street emptied into the river at Pearl.

In the end of the 17th century the tip of Manhattan Island had become such a busy shipping area that wharves and landfill extended the shoreline. By 1766 a strip of land two blocks deep had been added to the city.

In the 18th century wealthy homes, warehouses and some combined business and residential structures were located here. Pearl Street was widened in the 1820s, and residential buildings in the area gave way to more stores, factories and warehouses.

In the mid-19th century industry moved northward, and with the coming of steamships, shipping shifted to the wider Hudson River. In general, this area became a backwater area of stores, saloons and services for sailors. The Fraunces Tavern block buildings, however, continued as warehouses and light manufacturing plants.

After the 1929 stock market crash the docks were idle and more companies relocated to midtown. The area remained unchanged from the mid-19th century until the late 1950s, when a new construction boom began. Water Street was widened, and older blocks like this one came tumbling down to make way for new office towers.

The current buildings on the block represent a variety of eighteenth century styles, including Georgian, late Federal, Greek Revival, and Victorian.

ARCHAEOLOGICAL DIG   *Stop 17.*

85 Broad Street (east side of building, along Pearl Street)
Subway: N, R to Whitehall Street

The first large scale archaeological excavation in New York City was conducted on this block in 1979-80. The excavation yielded important cultural material from the 17th through 19th centuries, proving that significant archaeological deposits can be found in heavily developed urban areas. A number of wells, privies (or outhouses) and cisterns from the backyards of early houses, and the foundations and associated materials from the Lovelace Tavern were discovered. Excavations under Stone Street also uncovered a series of earth surfaces dating from the 17th through 19th centuries.

The archaeological exhibit in the plaza includes information about the Stadt Huys, Governor Lovelace's Tavern, an 18th century well, and Stone Street, a 17th century thoroughfare. The present day Pearl Street represents the approximate 17th century shoreline of the East River.

GOVERNOR LOVELACE'S TAVERN

The Lovelace Tavern was built in 1670 under the directive of Francis Lovelace, the second English Governor of New York, and remained in use until 1706, when it was torn down. It was owned by the British Crown and served as a temporary city hall for a short time after 1697, when the first City Hall, the Stadt Huys, was declared unsafe for use.

THE STADT HUYS

The Stadt Huys, or Dutch City Hall, was built as a tavern, the Stadt Herbergh (or City Inn), in 1641 by Director-General Kieft of the Dutch West India Company. When New Amsterdam became a municipality in 1653, the tavern was designated for use as the first City Hall, making it the center of governmental and political life in the Colony. It continued to serve this municipal function under both Dutch and English rule until it was declared unsafe for use in 1697, and was later torn down. The city government then convened at several taverns, including Lovelace Tavern, until the new City Hall was built at the northeast corner of Wall and Nassau Streets in 1699.

The Stadt Huys was built in typical 17th century Dutch style with a stepped gable. In the 17th century, the Stadt Huys was one of the largest public buildings in the city.

FIRST JEWISH SETTLEMENT   *Stop 18.*

South William Street & Mill Lane
Subway: IRT #4, 5 to Bowling Green

In 1654, the first Jews arrived in New Amsterdam, included in this group was Abraham de Lucena, who lived on this site until 1660. Asser Levy, butcher and first permanent settler, occupied a house in this lane. He and other Jews later had homes and shops on adjacent Stone Street.

The Jewish community worshipped on South William (then Mill) Street in a rented house until they erected the first synagogue in North America there in 1730. The plot of ground was purchased by Lewis and Mordecai Gomez, Jacob Franks, and Rodrigo Pacheco, trustees of Congregation Shearith Israel, on behalf of the colonial Jewish community. The building was completed by 1730 and consecrated by the congregation on April 8 of that year.The

Third Avenue "El" at Coentis Slip, circa 1904.

construction of the synagogue marked the establishment of a permanent place of worship for the community.

Look for the historic plaque on the corner of Mill Lane & South William Street.

VIETNAM VETERANS MEMORIAL   *Stop 19.*

Water Street & Coentis Slip
Subway: N, R to Whitehall Street

New York City's first Vietnam Memorial is located in Jeannette Park (between Water & South Streets). It consists of a glass-block wall inscribed with fragments of letters composed by soldiers-in-the-battlefields of Vietnam.

A FUN SKYSCRAPER   *Stop 20.*

127 John Street
Subway: IRT #2, 3, 4, 5 to Fulton Street

127 John Street was designed by Emery Roth & Sons. The lobby entrance is very unique. It was designed by Corchia de Harak and Howard Brandston. There are bright canvas canopies, scaffolding with brightly-painted street furniture, stage lighting, and a "space tunnel" made of corrugated metal tubes lined with blue neon lights. The elevators have bright red neon lights. It's almost like stepping into an X-ray machine. The mechanical floors (13th floor and penthouse level) consist of exposed ducts and pipes painted in bright primary colors, highlighted with flickering Christmas lights.They were designed by Pamela Waters.

Adjoining 127 John Street is the two-story John Street Restaurant which refused to sell to the developer. The architects therefore designed a unique camouflage device - a two story digital clock composed of sixty back-lighted numbered boxes.

SOUTH STREET SEAPORT

1. Titanic Memorial Lighthouse
2. Waterfront Photographer Gallery
3. Book & Chart Store
4. Curiousity Shop
5. Bowne & Co. Stationers
6. Museum Gallery
7. Melville Library
8. Small Craft Collection
9. Children's Center
10. Norway Galleries
11. Boat Building Shop
12. The Pilothouse
13. Pier 16 Ticketbooth
14. Container Store
15. Maritime Crafts Center
16. Fulton Fish Market
17. Museum Visitors' Center
18. Museum Shop
19. *Ambrose* lightship
20. *W.O Decker* tugboat
21. *Peking* sailing ship
22. *Pioneer* schooner
23. *Wavertree* tall ship (1885)
24. *Hart* steam ferry
25. *Howard* fishing schooner
A. Cannon's Walk block
B. Fulton Market Building
C. Pier 17
D. Schermerhorm Row
E. One Seaport Plaza
F. Front Street shops

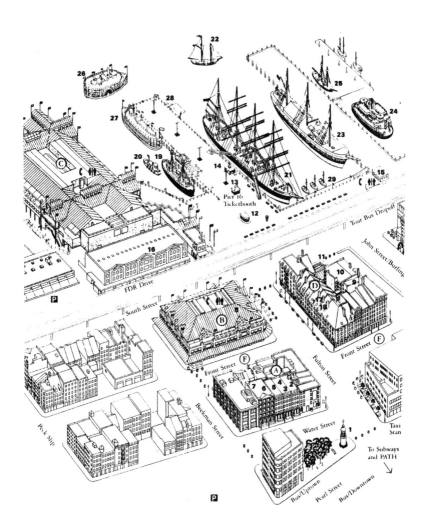

SOUTH STREET SEAPORT MUSEUM   *Stop 21.*

16 Fulton Street   Tel. (212)669-9400
Subway: IRT #2, 3, 4, 5 to Fulton Street

The South Street Seaport Museum celebrates old New York - the city that rose to world preeminence in the 19th century when South Street was known as the "Street of Ships." Vessels of every description lined these East River piers, and seamen, immigrants, merchants and tradesmen crowded these streets and buildings. Here was the center of the emerging city, the countinghouses and ship chandleries, the sail lofts, printing establishments, sailors' bars and flophouses that animated the extraordinary contribution of maritime enterprise to the growth of American commerce and culture.

The South Street Seaport is a kaleidoscope of galleries, boutiques and shops as well as a tantalizing array of restaurants, cafes, eateries and markets. Stand on the balcony of Pier 17 and watch the harbor traffic of tugs and tankers pass under the Brooklyn Bridge - watch street performers near the Fulton Market Building - enjoy concerts on the piers, holiday fireworks or the singing Christmas tree.

Catch the newest stars at Caroline's Comedy Club or see "The Seaport Experience" in New York's most unusual theater. Step aboard a 19th century tall ship, take a harbor cruise or come at 4:00 a.m. when the Fulton Fish Market comes to life.

SCHERMERHORN ROW

Fulton & South Street

The sloping roofs and tall chimneys of these early 19th century buildings form the architectural centerpiece of the Seaport. Built on speculation by Peter Schermerhorn, the block contains restaurants, a pub and many specialty stores. Once the whole neighborhood looked like this neat row of Federal and Greek Revival commercial

Woolworth Building was once the tallest building in the world.

buildings.

TITANIC MEMORIAL LIGHTHOUSE
Fulton & Pearl Streets

This unique memorial was erected in honor of those lost in the *Titanic* disaster of 1912.

ST. PAUL'S CHAPEL & GRAVEYARD   *Stop 22.*
Broadway & Fulton Street
Subway : IRT # 2, 3, 4, 5 to Fulton Street

St. Paul's Chapel was built in 1766 by Thomas McBean. Its model was James Gibbs's masterpiece, the Church of St. Martin's-in-the-Fields in London. Stone from the site (Manhattan schist) forms the walls that are quoined, columned, parapeted, pedimented, porched, and towered in brownstone.

Governor Clinton's and President Washington's pews are located in St. Paul's Chapel.

WOOLWORTH BUILDING   *Stop 23.*
233 Broadway
Subway: IRT #4, 5, 6 to Brooklyn Bridge

The Woolworth Building was erected by Frank Woolworth in 1913 as the headquarters tower for his chain of variety stores. Woolworth paid $13 million in cash for the 800-foot-high building which was once the tallest building in the world. It was designed in Neo-Gothic by Cass Gilbert. It was known as the "Cathedral of Commerce."

In the magnificent three-story lobby are caricatures in bas-relief of Frank Woolworth counting nickels and dimes, of Cass Gilbert holding a model of the building, of the renting agent closing a deal, and of others involved in the creation of the building.

CITY HALL   *Stop 24.*

Broadway & Park Row
Subway: IRT #4, 5, 6 to Brooklyn Bridge

City Hall was built in 1811 and was designed by Joseph F. Mangin and John McComb. This was one of the northernmost buildings in New York when it was constructed. The city-fathers felt that the city would not expand any further so they designed the front and sides façades in marble but the back of City Hall was faced with brownstone to save money.

The central hall, with its twin spiral, self-supporting marble stairs under a dome, is one of the finest public interiors. The Governor's Room was originally for his use when visiting New York City. It is now a portrait gallery.

TWEED COURTHOUSE   *Stop 25.*

52 Chambers Street
Subway: IRT # 4, 5, 6 to Brooklyn Bridge

The Tweed Ring was involved in the construction of this building located just behind City Hall. It cost anywhere from $10 to $14 million to construct this building. This was an excellent example of graft. Carpenters received $360,747 for a month's work and plasterers received $2,870,464 for a month's work!

SURROGATE'S COURT   *Stop 26.*

31 Chambers Street
Subway: IRT #4, 5, 6 to Brooklyn Bridge

This building, located across the street from the Tweed Courthouse, has been compared to a miniature version of the Paris Opera House. It was designed in the Beaux-Arts style in 1911 by John R. Thomas, Horgan & Slattery.

New York's City Hall was built in 1811

MUNICIPAL BUILDING   *Stop 27.*

1 Centre Street
Subway: IRT #4, 5, 6 to Brooklyn Bridge

This magnificent skyscraper does not overwhelm the nearby City Hall. It was designed in 1914 by McKim, Mead & White. It is one of the few buildings that has a subway station running within its steel and concrete foundation. Chambers Street once continued "through" the building, under its glorious arch. The vaulted ceiling in the exterior promenade was designed by Guastavino.

The castle-like pinnacles consisting of colonnaded towers are surmounted by Adolph Weinman's statue "Civic Fame." The Municipal Building is presently undergoing a major "face-lift." The top floors house the radio and television stations WNYC - Channel 31, the Municipal Broadcasting System.

BROOKLYN BRIDGE   *Stop 28.*

City Hall Park (Manhattan) to Cadman Plaza (Brooklyn)
Subway: IRT #4, 5, 6 to Brooklyn Bridge

The Brooklyn Bridge was opened in 1883. It took sixteen years to build and cost the lives of more than twenty people, including that of its designer, John A. Roebling. It was completed by his son, Washington A. Roebling. It is one of the most beautiful bridges in the world. It connected two independent cities, New York and Brooklyn. Brooklyn became part of New York City in 1898. The Gothic towers of the Brooklyn Bridge were the tallest structures in the city at the time of their construction. The skyscrapers were not built until the late 1880s.

Be sure to take a leisurely stroll across the Brooklyn Bridge. The pedestrian walkways can be reached from the IRT subway passageways.

The Municipal Building was designed by McKim, Mead & White.

Places to Visit

Manhattan

AMERICAN CRAFT MUSEUM
40 West 53rd Street   Tel. (212) 956-6047   (closed Mondays)
Subway: E, F Train to Fifth Avenue
AMERICAN MUSEUM OF NATURAL HISTORY
Central Park West & 79th Street   Tel. (212) 769-5920
Subway: B, C Train to 81st Street
ASIA SOCIETY GALLERIES
725 Park Avenue   Tel. (212) 288-6400   (closed Mondays)
Subway: IRT #6 to 68th Street
AT&T INFO QUEST CENTER
Madison Avenue & 56th Street   Tel. (212) 605-5555
 (closed Mondays)   Subway: E, F Train to Fifth Avenue
CARNEGIE HALL (Tours)
881 Seventh Avenue   Tel. (212) 903-9790
Subway: N, R to 57th Street
CENTRAL PARK ZOO
Fifth Avenue & 64th Street   Tel. (212) 861-6030
Subway: N, R to Fifth Avenue
CHILDREN'S MUSEUM OF MANHATTAN
212 West 83rd Street   Tel. (212) 721-1234   (closed Mondays)
Subway: IRT #1/9 to 86th Street
CHINA INSTITUTE IN AMERICA
125 East 65th Street   Tel. (212) 744-8181
Subway: N, R to Fifth Avenue

CITY HALL (Governor's Room)
Broadway & Murray Street   Tel. (212) 669-4506
(closed weekends)   Subway: IRT # 4, 5, 6 to Brooklyn Bridge
THE CLOISTERS
Fort Tryon Park   Tel. (212) 923-3700   (closed Mondays)
Subway: A Train to 190th Street
CON EDISON CONSERVATION CENTER
Lexington Avenue & 42nd Street   Tel. (212) 599-3435
(closed Sundays & Mondays)
Subway: IRT #4, 5, 6 to Grand Central Station
CON EDISON ENERGY MUSEUM
145 East 14th Street   Tel. (212) 460-6244
(closed Sundays & Mondays)
Subway: IRT #4, 5, 6 to Union Square
COOPER-HEWETT MUSEUM
2 East 91st Street   Tel. (212) 860-6868   (closed Mondays)
Subway: IRT #4, 5, 6 to 86th Street
EMPIRE STATE BUILDING (Observation Deck)
350 Fifth Avenue   Tel. (212) 736-3100
Subway: N, R to 34th Street
FEDERAL HALL NATIONAL MUSEUM
26 Wall Street   Tel. (212) 264-8711   (closed weekends)
Subway: IRT #2, 3, 4, 5 to Wall Street
FORBES MAGAZINE GALLERIES
62 Fifth Avenue   Tel. (212) 206-5548
 (closed Sundays, Mondays & Thursdays)
Subway: IRT #4, 5, 6 to Union Square
FRAUNCES TAVERN MUSEUM
54 Pearl Street   Tel. (212) 425-1776   (closed Saturdays)
Subway: N, R to Whitehall Street

FRICK COLLECTION

1 East 70th Street   Tel. (212) 288-0700   (closed Mondays)

Subway: IRT #6 to 68th Street

GRANT'S TOMB NATIONAL MEMORIAL

Riverside Drive & 122nd Street   Tel. (212) 666-1640

(closed Mondays & Tuesdays)

 Subway: IRT #1/9 to 116th Street

GRACIE MANSION (Tours)

East End Avenue & 88th Street   Tel. (212) 570-4751

Subway: IRT #4, 5, 6 to 86th Street

GUINNESS WORLD RECORDS EXHIBIT HALL

350 Fifth Avenue   Tel. (212) 947-2335

Subway: B, D, F, Q to 34th Street

GUGGENHEIM MUSEUM

Fifth Avenue & 88th Street   Tel. (212) 360-3500

(closed Mondays)

Subway: IRT #4, 5, 6 to 86th Street

HAMILTON GRANGE NATIONAL MEMORIAL

287 Convent Avenue   Tel. (212) 283-5154

(closed Mondays & Tuesdays)

Subway: IRT #1/9 to 145th Street

HAYDEN PLANETARIUM

Columbus Avenue & 81st Street   Tel. (212) 769-5920

Subway: B, C to 81st Street

HISPANIC SOCIETY OF AMERICA

Broadway & 155th Street   Tel. (212) 926-2234   (closed Mondays)

Subway: IRT # 1/9 to 157th Street

IBM GALLERY OF SCIENCE & ART

Madison Avenue & 56th Street   Tel. (212) 407-6100

(closed Mondays)   Subway: E, F Train to Fifth Avenue

INTERNATIONAL CENTER OF PHOTOGRAPHY (ICP)

Fifth Avenue & 94th Street   Tel (212) 860-1777

(closed Mondays)   Subway: IRT #6 to 96th Street

(Midtown Branch)

77 West 45th Street   Tel. (212) 869-2159   (closed Sundays)

Subway: B, D, F, Q to 47th-50th Streets, Rockefeller Center

U.S.S. INTREPID SEA-AIR-SPACE MUSEUM

Hudson River & 46th Street   Tel. (212) 245-2533

(closed Mondays & Tuesdays)

Subway: Any train to 42nd Street, then M42 bus

JEWISH MUSEUM

Fifth Avenue & 92nd Street   Tel. (212) 860-1888

(closed Fridays & Saturdays)

Subway: IRT # 4, 5, 6 to 86th Street

AUNT LEN'S DOLL & TOY MUSEUM

6 Hamilton Terrace   Tel. (212) 281-4143 (by appointment only)

Subway: IRT #1/9 to 145th Street

LIBRARY & MUSEUM OF THE PERFORMING ARTS

111 Amsterdam Avenue   Tel. (212) 870-1630   (closed Sundays)

Subway: IRT #1/9 to 66th Street

LINCOLN CENTER FOR THE PERFORMING ARTS (Tours)

140 West 65th Street   Tel. (212) 877-1800

Subway: IRT #1/9 to 66th Street

LOWER EAST SIDE TENEMENT MUSEUM

97 Orchard Street   Tel. (212) 431-0233

Subway: F Line to Delancey Street

METROPOLITAN MUSEUM OF ART

Fifth Avenue & 82nd Street   Tel. (212) 535-7710

(closed Mondays) Subway: IRT # 4, 5, 6 to 86th Street

METROPOLITAN OPERA (Backstage Tours)

Columbus Avenue & 65th Street   Tel. (212) 582-3512

Subway: IRT # 1/9 to 66th Street

MORRIS-JUMEL MANSION
1765 Jumel Terrace   Tel. (212) 923-8008   (closed Mondays)
Subway: IRT #1/9 to 157th Street

MUSEUM OF BROADCASTING
1 East 53rd Street   Tel. (212) 752-7684
 (closed Sundays & Mondays)
Subway: E, F Train to Fifth Avenue

MUSEUM OF HOLOGRAPHY
11 Mercer Street   Tel. (212) 925-0526   (closed Mondays)
Subway: N, R to Canal Street

MUSEUM OF MODERN ART
11 West 53rd Street   Tel. (212) 708-9480   (closed Wednesdays)
Subway: E, F Train to Fifth Avenue

MUSEUM OF THE AMERICAN INDIAN
Broadway & 155th Street   Tel. (212) 283-2420   (closed Mondays)
Subway: IRT #1/9 to 157th Street

MUSEUM OF THE CITY OF NEW YORK
Fifth Avenue & 103rd Street   Tel. (212) 534-1672
(closed Mondays)   Subway: IRT #6 to 103rd Street

NATIONAL ACADEMY OF DESIGN
Fifth Avenue & 89th Street   Tel. (212) 369-4880
(closed Mondays)   Subway: IRT #4, 5, 6 to 86th Street

NBC TOURS
30 Rockefeller Plaza   Tel. (212) 664-7174
Subway: B, D, F, Q to 47th-50th Streets, Rockefeller Center

NEW MUSEUM OF CONTEMPORARY ART
583 Broadway   Tel. (212) 219-1222
(closed Mondays & Tuesdays)
Subway: IRT #6 to Spring Street

NEW YORK CITY FIRE MUSEUM
278 Spring Street   Tel. (212) 691-1303   (closed Sundays)
Subway: IRT #1/9 to Canal Street

NEW YORK HISTORICAL SOCIETY
170 Central Park West   Tel. (212) 873-3400   (closed Mondays)
Subway: B, C Train to 81st Street

NEW YORK PUBLIC LIBRARY
Fifth Avenue & 42nd Street   Tel. (212) 930-0800
(closed Sundays)   Subway: B, D, F, Q to 42nd Street

NEW YORK STOCK EXCHANGE
20 Broad Street   Tel. (212) 656-5167   (closed weekends)
Subway: IRT #2, 3, 4, 5 to Wall Street

92ND STREET YMHA - PERFORMING ARTS CENTER
Lexington Avenue & 92nd Street   Tel. (212) 996-1105
Subway: IRT #4, 5, 6 to 86th Street

PIERPONT MORGAN LIBRARY
29 East 36th Street   Tel. (212) 685-0610   (closed Mondays)
Subway: IRT #6 to 33rd Street

POLICE ACADEMY MUSEUM
235 East 20th Street   Tel. (212) 477-9753   (closed weekends)
Subway: IRT #6 to 23rd Street

RADIO CITY MUSIC HALL - Backstage Tours
Sixth Avenue & 50th Street   Tel. (212) 757-3100
Subway: B, D, F, Q to 47th-50th Streets, Rockefeller Center

THEODORE ROOSEVELT BIRTHPLACE
28 East 20th Street   Tel. (212) 260-1616
(closed Mondays & Tuesdays)
Subway: IRT #6 to 23rd Street

ABIGAIL ADAMS SMITH MUSEUM
421 East 61st Street   Tel. (212) 838-6878
(closed weekends & August)
Subway: N, R to Lexington Avenue

SOUTH STREET SEAPORT MUSEUM
16 Fulton Street   Tel. (212) 669-9424
Subway: IRT #2, 3, 4, 5 to Fulton Street

STATUE OF LIBERTY

Liberty Island   Tel. (212) 363-3267

Ferry Information   Tel. (212) 269-5755

Subway: N, R to Whitehall Street

UKRAINIAN MUSEUM

203 Second Avenue   Tel. (212) 228-0110

(closed Mondays & Tuesdays)

Subway: IRT #4, 5, 6 to Union Square

UNITED NATIONS HEADQUARTERS

First Avenue & 46th Street   Tel. (212) 963-4440

(closed Sundays in winter)

Subway: IRT #4, 5, 6, 7 to Grand Central Station

WHITNEY MUSEUM OF AMERICAN ART

Madison Avenue & 75th Street   Tel.(212) 570-3676

(closed Mondays)   Subway: IRT #6 to 77th Street

WHITNEY MUSEUM AT EQUITABLE CENTER

787 Seventh Avenue   Tel. (212) 554-1113   (closed Sundays)

Subway:N, R to 49th Street

WHITNEY MUSEUM AT PHILIP MORRIS

120 Park Avenue   Tel. (212) 878-2550   (closed Sundays)

Subway: IRT #4, 5, 6, 7 to Grand Central Station

WHITNEY MUSEUM DOWNTOWN

Federal Reserve Plaza

  33 Maiden Lane   Tel. (212) 943-5655   (closed weekends)

Subway: IRT #2, 3, 4, 5 to Fulton Street

WORLD FINANCIAL CENTER (Winter Garden)

West & Liberty Streets   Tel. (212) 945-0505

Subway: IRT #1/9 to Cortlandt Street

WORLD TRADE CENTER (Observation Deck)

2 World Trade Center   Tel. (212) 466-7397

Subway: IRT #1/9 to Cortlandt Street

YESHIVA UNIVERSITY MUSEUM
2520 Amsterdam Avenue   Tel. (212) 960-5400
(closed Mondays, Fridays & Saturdays)
Subway: IRT #1/9 to 181st Street

Brooklyn

BROOKLYN BOTANICAL GARDEN
1000 Washington Avenue   Tel. (718) 622-4433
 (closed Mondays)
Subway: IRT #2, 3, 4 to Eastern Parkway
BROOKLYN CHILDREN'S MUSEUM
145 Brooklyn Avenue   Tel. (718) 735-4432   (closed Tuesdays)
Subway: IRT #3, 4 to Kingston Avenue
BROOKLYN HISTORICAL SOCIETY
128 Pierrepont Street   Tel. (718) 624-0890
Subway: IRT #2, 3, 4, 5 to Borough Hall
BROOKLYN MUSEUM
200 Eastern Parkway   Tel. (718) 638-5000   (closed Tuesdays)
Subway: IRT #2, 3, 4 to Eastern Parkway
HARBOR DEFENSE MUSEUM OF NEW YORK CITY
Fort Hamilton (101st Street Gate)   Tel. (718) 630-4349
(closed Tuesdays & Wednesdays)
Subway: R Train to 95th Street
LEFFERT'S HOMESTEAD
Flatbush Avenue, north of Empire Boulevard
Tel. (718) 768-2300
Subway: D, Q Train to Prospect Park
NEW YORK AQUARIUM
Surf Avenue & West 8th Street   Tel (718) 265-FISH
Subway: D, F Train to West 8th Street

NEW YORK CITY TRANSIT MUSEUM
Boerum Place & Schermerhorn Street   Tel. (718) 330-3060
(closed Sundays)
Subway: IRT #2, 3, 4, 5 to Borough Hall
ROTUNDA GALLERY
Brooklyn War Memorial at Cadman Plaza West
Tel. (718) 875-4031
Subway: IRT #2, 3, 4, 5 to Borough Hall

Queens

AMERICAN MUSEUM OF THE MOVING IMAGE
35th Avenue & 36th Street   Tel. (718) 784-0077
(closed Mondays & Tuesdays)
Subway: N Train to 36th Avenue
JAMAICA ARTS CENTER
161-04 Jamaica Avenue   Tel. (718) 658-7400
(closed Sundays & Mondays)
Subway: E Train to Jamaica Center
NEW YORK HALL OF SCIENCE
47-01 111th Street   Flushing Meadow Park
Tel. (718) 699-0005   (closed Mondays & Tuesdays)
Subway: IRT #7 to 111th Street
NOGUCHI GARDEN MUSEUM
32-37 Vernon Boulevard   Tel. (718) 204-7088
(closed December-March)
Subway: N Train to Broadway
QUEENS BOTANICAL GARDEN
43-50 Main Street   Tel. (718) 866-3800
Subway: IRT #7 to Main Street

QUEENS COUNTY FARM MUSEUM

73-50 Little Neck Parkway   Tel. (718) 347-FARM

(open Saturdays & Sundays)

Subway: IRT #7 to Main Street, then bus Q44 & Q44A

QUEENS HISTORICAL SOCIETY

143-35 37th Avenue   Tel. (718) 939-0647

Subway: IRT #& to Main Street

QUEENS MUSEUM

Flushing Meadow Park - New York City Building

Tel. (718) 592-2405   (closed Mondays)

Subway: IRT #7 to Willets Point - Shea Stadium

TERNBACH MUSEUM OF QUEENS COLLEGE

65-30 Kissena Boulevard   Tel. (718) 520-7129

(closed Tuesdays, Fridays & Sundays)

Subway: IRT #7 to Main Street,

then bus Q44 to Union Turnpike

The Bronx

BARTOW-PELL MANSION

Shore Road (Pelham Bay Park)   Tel. (212) 885-1461

Subway: IRT #6 to Pelham Bay Park then bus

BRONX MUSEUM OF THE ARTS

1040 Grand Concourse   Tel. (212) 681-6000   (closed Fridays)

Subway: C, D Train to 167th Street

THE BRONX ZOO

Tel. (212) 367-1010

Subway: IRT #2 to Pelham Parkway

CITY ISLAND HISTORICAL NAUTICAL MUSEUM

190 Fordham Road

Subway: IRT #6 to Pelham Bay Park

ENRICO FERMI CULTURAL CENTER

Belmont Library

Hughes Avenue & East 186th Street   Tel. (212) 933-6410

Subway: C, D Train to Fordham Road

HALL OF FAME NATIONAL MEMORIAL

Bronx Community College

University Avenue & Hall of Fame Terrace

 Tel. (212) 220-6450

Subway: IRT #4 to Burnside Avenue

MUSEUM OF BRONX HISTORY

Bainbridge Avenue & 208th Street   Tel. (212) 881-8900

Subway: D Train to 205th Street

MUSEUM OF MIGRATING PEOPLE

Truman High School

Baychester Avenue & Donizetti Place   Tel. (212) 379-1600

Subway: IRT #5 to Gun Hill Road

NEW YORK BOTANICAL GARDENS

Tel. (212) 220-8700

Subway: C, D Train to Bedford Park Boulevard

NORTH WIND UNDERSEA MUSEUM

610 City Island Avenue   Tel. (212) 885-0701

Subway: IRT #6 to Pelham Bay Park

                then bus BX12 to City Island

EDGAR ALLAN POE COTTAGE

Grand Concourse & Kingsbridge Road

Tel. (212) 881-8900   (closed Mondays & Tuesdays)

Subway: C, D Train to Kingsbridge Road

VALENTINE-VARIAN HOUSE

Bainbridge Avenue & 208th Street   Tel. (212) 881-8900

Subway: D Train to 205th Street

WAVE HILL CENTER FOR THE PERFORMING ARTS
Independence Avenue & 249th Street   Tel. (212) 549-2055
Subway: IRT #1/9 to 242nd Street

Staten Island

SNUG HARBOR CULTURAL CENTER
1000 Richmond Terrace   Tel. (718) 448-5200
(closed Mondays & Tuesdays)   Bus: S1
STATEN ISLAND BOTANICAL GARDENS
1000 Richmond Terrace   Tel. (718) 273-8200
Bus: S1
STATEN ISLAND INSTITUTE OF ARTS & SCIENCES
75 Stuyvesant Place   Tel. (718) 727-1135   (closed Mondays)
Near Staten Island Ferry Terminal.
STATEN ISLAND ZOO
614 Broadway   Tel. (718) 442-3101   Bus: S107
MARCHAIS CENTER OF TIBETAN ART
338 Lighthouse Avenue   Tel. (718) 987-3478   Bus: S4, S113
RICHMONDTOWN RESTORATION
441 Clarke Avenue   Tel. (718) 351-1611
(closed Mondays & Tuesdays)   Bus: S4, S113

TOURS OF JEWISH NEW YORK CITY...

* Lower East Side
* Colonial Jewish New York
* Ellis Island
* Synagogues of New York
* Changing Neighborhoods of the City
* Chassidic Neighborhoods of Brooklyn
* Boat Tour of Jewish New York

Israelowitz Tours

P.O.Box 228 Brooklyn, New York 11229   Tel. (718) 951-7072

Israelowitz Publishing

P.O.Box 228   Brooklyn, New York 11229   Tel. (718) 951-7072

CATALOGUE

Lower East Side Guide
by Oscar Israelowitz
Paperback   5" x 7"   124 pages $4.95
(plus $2.00 shipping)   ISBN 0-961136-4-7

New York City Subway Guide
by Oscar Israelowitz
Paperback   5" x 8"   259 pages $6.95
(plus $2.00 shipping)   ISBN 0-961136-7-1

Guide to Jewish New York City
by Oscar Israelowitz
Paperback   5" x 7"   264 pages $9.95
(plus $2.00 shipping)   ISBN 1-878741-00-4

Guide to Jewish Europe
Western Europe Edition
by Oscar Israelowitz
Paperback 5" x 8" 320 pages $11.95
(plus $2.00 shipping) ISBN 0-9611036-1-2

Guide to Jewish Italy
by Annie Sacerdoti
Paperback 8" x 11" 199 pages $12.95
(plus $2.50 shipping) ISBN 0-9611036-3-9

Guide to Jewish Canada & U.S.A.
Volume I - Eastern Provinces
by Oscar Israelowitz
Paperback 5" x 8" 320 Pages $11.95
(plus $2.00 shipping) ISBN 0-9611036-8-X

Guide to Jewish U.S.A.
Volume II - South
by Oscar Israelowitz
Paperback 5" x 7" 175 pages $9.95
(plus $2.00 shipping) ISBN 0-961136-6-3

The Ellis Island Guide

with Lower Manhattan

by Oscar Israelowitz

Paperback 4" x 6" 164 pages $7.95
(plus $2.00 shipping) ISBN 1-878741-01-2

Flatbush Guide

by Oscar Israelowitz

Paperback 5" x 7" 111 pages $4.95
(plus $2.00 shipping) ISBN 0-9611036-9-8

EAT YOUR WAY THROUGH AMERICA & CANADA

A Kosher Dining Guide

by Oscar Israelowitz

Paperback 4" x 6" 164 pages $5.95
(plus $2.00 shipping) ISBN 1-878741-03-9

Index

NOTES

NOTES

NOTES

NOTES

NOTES

NOTES

NOTES

NOTES

NOTES

NOTES

NOTES

NOTES

NOTES

NOTES

NOTES

NOTES

NOTES

NOTES

NOTES

NOTES

NOTES

NOTES

NOTES

NOTES

NOTES

NOTES

NOTES